The Johnstown Flood, 1889

Dan Leathers

Mitchell Lane
PUBLISHERS

P.O. Box 196
Hockessin, Delaware 19707
Visit us on the web: www.mitchelllane.com
Comments? email us:
mitchelllane@mitchelllane.com

Mitchell Lane PUBLISHERS

Copyright © 2008 by Mitchell Lane Publishers. All rights reserved. No part of this book may be reproduced without written permission from the publisher. Printed and bound in the United States of America.

Printing   1   2   3   4   5   6   7   8   9

A Robbie Reader/Natural Disasters

Library of Congress Cataloging-in-Publication Data
Leathers, Dan.
  The Johnstown Flood, 1889 / by Dan Leathers.
    p. cm. — (A Robbie Reader. Natural disasters)
  Includes bibliographical references and index.
  Audience: Grades K-3.
  ISBN 978-1-58415-570-6 (library bound)
  1. Floods—Pennsylvania—Johnstown (Cambria County)—History—19th century—Juvenile literature. 2. Johnstown (Cambria County, Pa.)—History—19th century—Juvenile literature. I. Title.
F159.J7L43 2008
974.8'77041—dc22

2007000799

ABOUT THE AUTHOR: Dr. Daniel Leathers has been fascinated with the earth's environment since childhood. This fascination has developed into a career, teaching about and researching our amazing planet. He attended Lycoming College and the Pennsylvania State University, earning degrees in physics, meteorology, and geography. He currently teaches in the Geography Department at the University of Delaware. He is the author of more than 35 scientific articles and numerous popular publications. He lives in the Amish country of Pennsylvania with his wife and two daughters.

PHOTO CREDITS: Cover, pp. 8, 12—L. Kenneth Townsend; pp. 1, 6, 17, 18, 21, 23, 24—Library of Congress; pp. 4, 11, 15—Johnstown Area Heritage Association; p. 14—Jupiter Images; p. 16—W. Rogers; p. 21—Mr. Steve Nicklas/NOAA National Weather Service Collection; p. 27—NASA.

PLB

TABLE OF CONTENTS

Words in **bold** type can be found in the glossary.

Stony Creek flows through Johnstown, Pennsylvania. Johnstown was a growing city of about 30,000 people before the flood swept through in May 1889.

Gertrude's Story

Gertrude's father yelled, "Run for your lives. Follow me straight to the hill. Don't go back for anything!"

This was the first time that six-year-old Gertrude Quinn knew that anything was wrong. Her **nursemaid** grabbed her and ran out of the house and toward the street. But when they reached the street, they saw a wall of water coming toward them. The nursemaid and Gertrude turned back to the house.

They ran quickly up to the third floor of their beautiful home, one of the nicest in Johnstown, Pennsylvania. They thought if they were on the top floor of their house, they would be safe. They were wrong.

Two large brick buildings in Johnstown that were severely damaged in the flood. The floodwaters ripped the walls right off, and anyone in those rooms would likely have been swept away.

They heard people on the street below running and screaming. Gertrude's house began to shake, and it came apart. Gertrude was suddenly under the water. She fought hard to swim back to the surface. Once her head was clear, she climbed on top of a mattress that was floating by.

The body of a dead horse bumped into the mattress and almost knocked Gertrude into the swirling flood. She screamed for help as she floated farther and farther along. Finally she floated near a house roof carrying twenty people. A brave man jumped off the roof to help the little girl. Now they were both on the mattress.

After a short time, they came close to a hill that was above the water. The man threw Gertrude to some other men who were safe on the hill. These men caught Gertrude and took care of her.

Gertrude's father found her a day later. They had been caught in the great Johnstown flood!

An L. Kenneth Townsend painting of the South Fork Dam before it collapsed. The dam was made of soil and rocks. It was about 72 feet high and nearly 900 feet long.

What Caused the Johnstown Flood?

Thursday, May 30, 1889, started out as any normal day for the people of Johnstown, Pennsylvania. By that evening, rain had begun to fall in the nearby mountains. No one expected it to rain as hard as it did that night. It rained more than 6 inches during the night, and it kept falling the next morning. Streams began to spill over their banks. In some places, nearly 10 inches of rain fell in less than 24 hours.

The people in Johnstown had been through many floods before. Two rivers—Little Conemaugh (KAH-neh-maw) River and Stony Creek—meet in the town. When the people of Johnstown woke up on Friday, May 31, 1889, they were not very worried that the two rivers in their town were flooding. This happened all the time. But some people in Johnstown were worried about a dam, about 14 miles away, in the mountains east of town. They worried that the South Fork Dam may break and send water down the valley of the Little Conemaugh River into Johnstown.

The dam was made of dirt, clay, and stones. It was 72 feet high and as long as three football fields. It held back the water of Lake Conemaugh, a huge body of water.

More than six streams ran into the lake to keep it filled. It was between two and three miles long, one mile wide, and nearly 70 feet deep in some places. The lake was owned by people from Pittsburgh, Pennsylvania, who used it for fishing and boating. The South Fork Dam was the only thing between all this water and the city of Johnstown.

The rainstorm that hit western Pennsylvania on May 30 and 31, 1889, was

The South Fork Dam had to be large to hold back all the water in Lake Conemaugh.

one of the worst in history. Because the rain fell so hard and so fast, most of it ran across the ground and into the streams that emptied into Lake Conemaugh. As the rain fell hour after hour, the lake filled up more and more until it was up to the top of the dam.

A painting by L. Kenneth Townsend shows the South Fork Dam just as it began to fall apart. The water is running over the middle of the dam, cutting a huge hole for floodwaters to burst through.

The South Fork Dam Breaks

By Friday morning, it was clear that the South Fork Dam was in trouble. The water in Lake Conemaugh was rising at a rate of one inch every 10 minutes, and it was already nearing the top of the dam. The men in charge of the dam were working very hard to save it and keep it from breaking.

Near noon, the water began to flow over the dam's rim. During the next three hours, it washed out a hole near the center of the dam. The hole grew larger and larger. There was nothing that anyone could do to stop it. At about 3:10 P.M. on Friday, May 31, the entire dam collapsed. The water from Lake Conemaugh rushed down the valley of the

A view of Niagara Falls on a normal day. Many scientists believe that the water flowing over the South Fork Dam was equal to the water that flows over Niagara Falls.

Little Conemaugh River. Some scientists say that the amount of water that burst through the dam was as great as the amount that goes over Niagara Falls.

It took only about 40 minutes for all the water to drain from Lake Conemaugh after the dam burst. The people in Johnstown had no idea what was coming.

The wall of water that rushed out of Lake Conemaugh was nearly 40 feet high as it tore through the valley below. As it traveled, it picked up huge amounts of **debris**. Trees, pieces of buildings, large stones, dead animals, and dead people became part of the moving wall of water. It took about one hour for the water to move from the lake to Johnstown. This means it was moving at an average speed of about 15 miles per hour. However, in some places it was moving as fast as 40 miles per hour.

Imagine seeing a wall of water and debris moving toward you that fast. What a frightening

The path of the Johnstown Flood as it tore through the city. When the waters reached the city, it spread out in all directions.

CHAPTER THREE

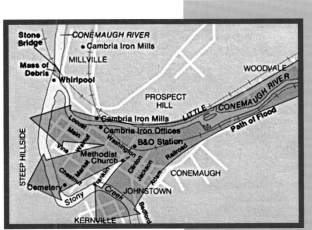

An artist's idea of Johnstown as the debris-filled floodwave swept through town. The artist, W. Rogers, used descriptions from survivors to draw this picture.

experience it must have been for everyone in the path of the flood. One person who saw the water crashing through town was a **minister** named David Beale. The Reverend Beale said the floodwaters "looked like an avalanche: an enormous wall of water thundering down the mountain into the valley community, carrying debris, livestock, train cars and human beings."

The Reverend wrote a lot about the Johnstown flood. However, many of his writings were lost for over 115 years. In 2006, they were found in Philadelphia. As historians began reading his lost diaries, they started to understand the flood much better.

After the South Fork Dam collapsed, Lake Conemaugh was empty.

An upturned house and tree in a tangled mess. Some houses were shattered by the floodwaters. Others rotted away after the flood receded.

The Flood Reaches Johnstown

The wall of water from the South Fork Dam reached Johnstown at about four o'clock on Friday afternoon. Most of the 30,000 people in Johnstown never knew that there was any danger. The first sign of trouble was a low rumbling sound that became louder and louder. Most people described the sound of the rushing water as being like thunder.

Many people hurried outside their homes just in time to see the wall of water, now at least 40 feet high, hurtling toward their neighbor-hoods. The water was so filled with **wreckage** that they could only see trees, pieces of houses, and other debris at the head of the wave. When they saw the water coming, most people in town either ran to the upper floors of their homes or left their houses to run to higher ground. The floodwaters quickly shattered most of the buildings in Johnstown. The wood became rafts that people held on to for survival.

In the first fifteen minutes after the wave hit Johnstown, many people died. Survivors

Main and Clinton Streets were completely devastated. Mounds of debris towered where buildings once stood.

The stone bridge (background) kept the mountain of debris from floating completely out of town.

had horrifying stories to tell about those awful minutes after the wave hit their homes. Anna Fenn was at her home with her seven children when the flood wave hit. She did her best to hold on to her children as the water filled their house. One by one, each child was separated from her and drowned. Anna Fenn's husband

21

also drowned in the flood. Anna lost her entire family within minutes. She survived and lived another 39 years.

Sixteen-year-old Victor Heiser watched as the flood washed away his parents and their home. He was in the family's barn when the wave hit. He rode the flood wave on the roof of the barn for a very long time. He finally was able to jump off and find safety in the attic of a house with 19 other people. Victor would later become a doctor who would find a treatment for the disease **leprosy**. Many doctors believe that this treatment has saved millions of lives in the last 100 years. Thankfully, Victor Heiser survived the Johnstown flood.

The wall of water was not the only danger in Johnstown. A huge stone bridge crossed the Conemaugh River at the west end of town. This bridge had been built by the Pennsylvania Railroad for their trains to cross the river. When the debris-filled water hit this bridge, the bridge acted like a dam. All the debris in the water, with the many people holding on to

The stone bridge days after the flood. Many people died in the fire that erupted at the stone bridge. Note the huge piles of wreckage that had yet to be cleared.

floating house pieces, were caught up in a huge, tangled pile at the bridge. Many of these people became trapped. In a very short time, the pile of wreckage caught on fire. It burned throughout the night, killing those who were trapped at the bridge. The city of Johnstown had been destroyed in a matter of a few hours.

Clara Barton, the founder of the American Red Cross. Barton and the Red Cross arrived in Johnstown five days after the flood and were a huge help as the city began to rebuild.

The Nation Helps Johnstown

It didn't take long for the rest of the United States to find out about the disaster in Johnstown. Although there were no radios, televisions, cell phones, or computers in 1889, there were **telegraphs** and newspapers. People from the area around Johnstown who knew about the disaster raced to nearby towns to have telegraph operators call for help from the rest of the country. Rescuers arrived in Johnstown very quickly, mostly by train.

One of the groups that helped was the new American Red Cross. Clara Barton, who founded the Red Cross, was in Johnstown five days after the flood occurred. Over the next five months, she and other Red Cross workers

25

helped the Johnstown survivors rebuild their homes and their lives.

The U.S. government also sent soldiers, supplies, and money to help rebuild Johnstown. Nearly $4 million was collected from people in the United States and eighteen other countries to help the people in the Conemaugh Valley. It took a long time and a lot of hard work, but Johnstown was slowly able to recover from the devastating flood.

In all, 2,209 people died in the Johnstown flood. Nearly 400 of these were children. It is still one of the worst natural disasters that has ever hit the United States. An unusual rainstorm and a poorly **maintained** dam worked together to cause this loss of life and property.

Scientists and engineers learned many valuable lessons from this event. They learned how to construct better and safer dams. They also learned that they must design dams and other structures to hold up under the worst that nature has to offer. Hopefully, this will be a lesson that will never be forgotten.

In 2007, the Three Gorges Dam in China was the largest dam in the world. It is constructed of concrete and steel and is much stronger than a dam made of soil and rocks.

CHRONOLOGY

1839   Work begins on the South Fork Dam. The dam is not finished until 1852.

1880   Dam is rebuilt by the South Fork Fishing and Hunting Club.

1889

May 28   A strong storm forms in the Great Plains of the United States. It begins to move toward Pennsylvania.

May 30   Rain begins to fall in Johnstown during the evening.

May 31   Rain falls heavily in the mountains around Johnstown overnight and through the morning.

12:00 P.M. Water begins to flow over the top of the South Fork Dam. Many people realize the dam is doomed.

3:10 P.M. South Fork Dam collapses in a matter of seconds. Water from Lake Conemaugh starts moving toward Johnstown.

4:07 P.M. A wall of water and debris 40 feet high reaches Johnstown and destroys the city in minutes.

Evening Debris at Pennsylvania Railroad stone bridge catches fire. Up to 80 trapped flood survivors die in the fire.

June 1   First relief workers arrive to aid survivors.

June 5   Clara Barton and the American Red Cross arrive to help survivors. The Red Cross works in Johnstown for the next five months.

OTHER DEADLY U.S. FLOODS

1913   March: Over 700 die in Ohio and Indiana as five days of extremely heavy rain on already wet ground causes almost all the rivers in the two states to flood.

1927   April: The Mississippi River floods after heavy winter and spring rains across the eastern half of the United States. Nearly all states along the Mississippi River are affected.

1936   March: Nearly 200 people die in flooding across Ohio, Pennsylvania, and West Virginia as heavy rain falls and melts very deep snow in the mountains.

1951 July: Kansas City and all of Missouri are hit by severe floods; 41 die as heavy rain falls across the state from July 9 to 13.

1969 January/February: Flooding in California leaves more than 100 dead as massive storms drop up to 50 inches of rain in the mountains of Southern California.

1972 September: Flooding in and around Rapid City, South Dakota, leaves 238 dead as more than 15 inches of rain fall in six hours.

1976 July: Flash flooding in Big Thompson Canyon, Colorado, results in 145 deaths. This flooding is caused by a thunderstorm that drops more than 12 inches of rain in a few hours in the mountains above the canyon.

1977 July: Johnstown, Pennsylvania, once again suffers a flooding disaster as nearly 12 inches of rain cause several local dams to burst; 76 people die in the flooding.

1993 June–August: Mississippi River flooding across the Midwest kills approximately 50 people when heavy thunderstorms strike nearly every day for more than six weeks.

1996 January: Melting mountain snows and heavy rain lead to severe flooding in northern Pennsylvania. At least 14 people are killed as water with temperatures near freezing roars through the mountain valleys near Williamsport, Pennsylvania.

2005 September: Hurricane Katrina hits the Mississippi and Louisiana coasts. Many people die from storm surge flooding. New Orleans, Louisiana, is flooded by Lake Pontchartrain when the levees break, leaving the city almost completely under water. More than 1,000 people die in the storm.

2007 August: At least 26 people die as rains brought by Tropical Storm Erin flood parts of Texas, Oklahoma, and Missouri. Thousands of homes and other buildings are destroyed.

FIND OUT MORE

Books

Gow, Mary. *The Johnstown Flood: The Day the Dam Burst.* Berkeley Heights, New Jersey: Enslow Publishers, 2003.

Gross, Virginia. *Once Upon America: The Day It Rained Forever.* New York: Puffin USA, 1993.

Nobleman, Marc. *We the People: The Johnstown Flood.* Mankato, Minnesota: Compass Point Books, 2005.

Walker, Paul. *Head for the Hills.* New York: Random House, 1993.

Works Consulted

McCullough, David. *The Johnstown Flood.* New York: Simon and Schuster, 1968.

McGough, Dr. Michael R. *The 1889 Flood in Johnstown, Pennsylvania.* Gettysburg, Pennsylvania: Thomas Publications, 2002.

New York Times. Johnstown Flood Articles: June 1, June 3, June 7, 1889.

Plushnick-Masti, Ramit. "Diaries Add Insight on Deadly Pa. Flood," Associated Press, May 29, 2007. http://www.abcnews4.com/news/stories/0507/426933.html

On the Internet

Johnstown Area Heritage Association http://www.jaha.org/

Johnstown Flood Museum http://www.jaha.org/FloodMuseum/oklahoma.html

Johnstown Flood National Memorial http://www.nps.gov/archive/jofl/home.htm

GLOSSARY

debris (duh-BREE)—What is left of something that has been broken into pieces or destroyed.

leprosy (LEP-ruh-see)—A long-lasting, contagious disease that affects the skin and nerves.

maintained (mayn-TAYND)—Kept in good shape or in good working order.

minister (MIH-nuh-ster)—A person who can lead a church.

nursemaid (NURS-mayd)—A woman or girl who is paid to take care of one or more children.

telegraph (TEH-lih-graf)—A way to send messages over long distances through a steel wire.

wreckage (REH-kidj)—The remains or pieces of something that has been wrecked.

INDEX